Accolades of
The Gentle Giant

The expression of my soul through free verses and rhyming poetry; from my soul to yours.

Forward

The Gentle Giant is the standard of the state of mind of my person of character and integrity. The Gentle Giant is for me to appreciate that rather I'm a son, nephew, father, uncle, or grandfather I understand I am the positive force of every situation even if it's to be silent and pray.

The Gentle Giant is a longsuffering loving man. The Gentle Giant is a humble man of character. The Gentle Giant is a place in a man's life when he comes to know himself for the person he is mentally, spiritually, and earnestly. It's the man to become within not the pride or arrogance we bolster on the outside.

TABLE OF CONTENTS

Devotions   2

Divine Sacrifice	3
My Life	4
My Master Plan	5
Charity	6
Cause & Effect	7
Stand	8
Superstar	9
I Say To Self	10
Me	11
Unbreakable	12
But a Champion	13
Humbly Speaking	14
Fearlessness	15
Respect	16
My Resolve	17

Be Peaceful	18
For The Future	19
Champion	20
Life	21
Peace Within	22
Pain In The Womb	23
I Am Alive	24
Being Better	25
I Celebrate Life	26
I Am	27
Practice Walking	28
I Am Champion	29
100%	30
As For Me	31
The Finisher	32
Nothing Shall Separate Me	33

Proverbs 34

Practice	35
Real	36

The Traveler In Me	37
Practice Love	39
Man I am	40
Ladders Stairs and Life	41
Choose Your Battles	42
Footnote	43
Survival	44
The Gamer	45
Self-Liberation	46
Failed Leadership	47
My Truth vs. Their Facts	48
The Sanity Of It	49
Plan Now For Your Future	50
Appreciate	51

My People, My People — 52

My People	53
I Am For my People	54
My Peoples Keeper	55
Understanding	56
Cares of our Mother	57

A Day in the Life Of......59

The Monuments Man	60
Distractions	61
Self can't lie to me	62
Grateful	63
This Moment	64
Within Me	65
Birthed New	66
I'll build my own ladder thank you	67
Anew	68
The Light Of A Man	69

Psalms of Bernon   71

Spiritual Bliss	72
You and My Days	74
Lost	75
My Mystic Beauty	76
UH!	78
The Thoughts of You	79

I Love You	80
Satisfied Jus Ti Fication	81
Yeah!	82
OK Daddy	83
To You	85
But I Still Care	86
Blind Presence	87
If You Let Me	88
I'll Tell You What	89
We Cool	91
Lustful Quarrel	92
If You Love Let Her Go	93
I Saw Your Soul (you missed me)	95
Self-Preservation	96
Broken for Peace	97
I'm Just Saying	98
Love Story	99
Who's The Dummy Now?	100
A Simple Care	102
My New Heart	103

My Visual	*104*
You	*105*
Indeed it's greater	*106*
All cause I flicker	*107*
My Passion Always	*109*
When I get a hold of you	*110*
If You Welcome Me	*112*
Soft as a whisper	*113*
Smile	*114*
I could kiss you there	*115*
Thunder!	*116*
All I want to do is love you	*117*

Devotions

Devotions

Devotions

Divine Sacrifice

Day 1

Without blessing humanity first there is no pleasing the creator. If we should treat any human being less than any of us would like to be treated and believe the love we have for our creator is justified and true, We Are A Liar because The Truth Is Not In Us.

We must appreciate the great sacrifice in offering up ourselves is to love and respect the liberties of each and every person in spite of who they are...not because of who they are.

Practice Practice Practice! Till the person you dream of becomes the person you are.

My Life

Day 2

Today, I have declared I have no enemies. I am at peace with the heavens. This world is my home and my life is the gift. I will cherish this gift. I will protect this gift, for this gift conceals my greatest assets. My spiritual being, my state of mind and my purpose. My life is divine and is concluded as perfection to Him who created me. Oh what a gift... My Life.

Practice Practice Practice! Till the person you dream of becomes the person you are.

My Master Plan

Day 3

I've been falsely accused... Judged! But I know a man.

I have been used and at times abused, but I know a man.

On this occasion, I have taken the liberty to reach within myself. I have accepted the opportunity to focus on my Master Plan. Rather than getting upset or falling into disenchantment. I will pick myself up, and I will live. I will live my beautiful, purposeful life beyond the ill wills around me. I will allow my soul to soar as eagles on high and I will reign. I will reign as a cloud of glory as my Master perfects His Master Plan through my life.

Practice Practice Practice! Till the person you dream of becomes the person you are.

Charity

Day 4

Because Bigot America has set the stage for me... I have a thousand reasons to do something stupid. And on second thought I have a thousand reasons to do something to the present bigots in America for hate crimes against humanity in this very instance of my life. BUT I have one reason to do the responsible thing. I have but one reason to respect myself, my family, my friends and my enemies. That reason is love. I will be the love that drives out hate, understanding that as Marcus Garvey, Dr. Martin Luther King Jr and Malcolm X never enjoyed the victories of their charity work. I may not either...that's fine. As long as I spend my life working for charity. Love is my reasoning.

Practice Practice Practice! Till the person you dream of becomes the person you are.

Cause & Effect

Day 5

Just like Yen and Yang, you can't have one without the other. However, I will add as I attempted to move forward through this life. I declare I will be the best man I can possibly be. I will strive for perfection though my good may be evil spoken of or even at times misunderstood. I will not quit...I will not give up! My Cause, My Effect, My Purpose, His Will... MY LIFE!

Practice... Practice... Practice! Till the person you dream of becomes the person you are.

Stand

Day 6

If all you can do is "stand", then stand and hope and love... These pure God given verbs will sustain you and comfort you with peace if you would just "STAND".

Practice Practice Practice! Till the person you dream of becomes the person you are.

Superstar

Day 7

For years, I have coined the phrase "I would whether look like I'm wrong then be Dead Right" or in this case fired...but right. Lol Today, it has been a great testament and understood proverb to my life. "Dear Abba Father continue to bless me generously to your glory." Therefore, I will stand courageously for righteousness by the power invested in me. I don't have anything to prove so I can't be baited into unhealthy compromising situations. I will fearlessly walk away to defy foolishness. I Am a Superstar!

Practice Practice Practice! Till the person you dream of becomes the person you are.

I Say To Self

Day 8

Let no man take your peace. Leave no woman to steal your joy. Protect and guard your state-of-mind with vigor. Look to be the best you, you can be in every situation. Even the storm has its purpose. In your deepest convictions, you must always deliver the greatest you, you will ever be, and being this is your true purpose. Because the sun will shine again and you owe it to yourself to be a prism of your splendor.

Practice Practice Practice! Till the person you dream of becomes the person you are.

Me

Day 9

If you leave me without, then I shall truly be without... you. However, I will still have me. The love, the joy and the power to hope that the best in me is just ahead. The great man I am is right here with me. Forever present as the air I breathe as the gravity that grounds me. Yes, because of you I may be without. Nevertheless, I am complete being right here with me.

Practice Practice Practice! Till the person you dream of becomes the person you are.

Unbreakable

Day 10

To be pulled in so many directions can make or break anyone. I refuse to "break". I choose to "make" the best out of every moment. The hurt that is inflicted upon me will not reflect through my life. The "power" invested in me will befall the pains of my sorrow. My love will secure my being as a man of hope, peace and integrity in spite of my battles.

Practice Practice Practice! Till the person you dream of becomes the person you are.

#StillIRise

But A Champion

Day 11

Winners win but CHAMPIONS... CHAMPIONS reign. Win lose or draw a CHAMPION is a CHAMPION is a CHAMPION. Character makes a champion while moments make a winner.

Practice Practice Practice! Till the person you dream of becomes the person you are.

Humbly Speaking

Day 12

Bitterness, a disposition one must not allow himself to fall into. The Champion is to train the mind to compete above the standards of this world. Remember "we are in this world but not of this world." As we define ourselves, we must accept the humanities of our brothers and sisters which we share this world with.

One must take heed that we cannot defy the humanities' of even ourselves though we strive for perfection it is certain we ourselves are yet human. We are all human.

Practice Practice Practice! Till the person you dream of becomes the person you are.

#HumblySpeaking

Fearlessness

Day 13

Be fearless, remove the mask and live above the person you want people to think you are. Be fearless! Practice Practice Practice! Till the person you dream of becomes the person you are.

Respect

Day 14

It is hard to give someone something they refuse to offer him/her-self. Just because a person doesn't respect him/herself doesn't give me an excuse to miss appropriate my liberties. Nevertheless, I will continue to be the person I dream of being, I will respect them too.

Practice Practice Practice! Till the person you dream of becomes the person you are.

My Resolve

Day 15

Today I have resolved; I have no enemies...no not one. As I am compelled to move forward fearlessly. I will not consider, except greater is He within me, far greater then hate, rage or even death. Far greater than even life. Therefore, I Love to Live.

Practice Practice Practice! Till the person you dream of becomes the person you are.

Be Peaceful

Day 16

The thing about peace is once you achieve it you will never put yourself in a position to lose it. You will fight for peace, and the thing is...all you have to do in your quest for peace is "be peaceful". All you have to do to defend your peace is "be peaceful". Consider nothing above your sound mind and accept nothing less than peace. Be the peace in every situation...

Practice Practice Practice! Till the person you dream of becomes the person you are.

For The Future

Day 17

Be careful what you do today may cost you your tomorrow. Be wise that your emotion at this moment doesn't devour your peace. I pray the decisions of this day be a stepping stone to your glorious future.

Practice Practice Practice! Till the person you dream of becomes the person you are.

Champion

Day 18

There is always one more victory in a CHAMPION.

Practice Practice Practice! Till the person you dream of becomes the person you are.

Life

Day 19

Life isn't always fair, sometimes it is simply not our fault yet, we must Practice being the person we dream of being even above the difficulties that press us out of our comforts. Because of the actions of others we all have suffered deplorable ramifications though we ourselves did not one thing to deserve the punishment. However, I am yet reminded that this life is worth living; we are the difference. We are purpose to make this life more palatable for everyone including ourselves.

Practice Practice Practice! Till the person you dream of becomes the person you are.

Peace Within

Day 20

That special effect of cares and concerns of one's greatness that escorts self-control, self-worth, and self-awareness. It's an unexplained action that causes people to respect you and others to envy you. It's the perfect champion you will ever know and the closest friend you will ever have. Peace within, that calm presence that's there when you have fallen that whispers, that urges you to rise and summit. It's that nudge that hints to you "one more mile", "one more time" when no-one else is around.

Peace within, that liberating revelation when you comprehend you don't have to take yourself so serious. Peace within, is when you establish yourself as a listener versus one who is quick to speak. Peace within, that perfection to understand all things at all times for the benefit of everyone involved is peace within.

Practice Practice Practice! Till the person you dream of becomes the person you are.

Pain In The Womb

Day 21

Why pain?! Pain is that deep sorrow that brings tears to my eyes. That emptiness of a Love once gone, lost passion and devastating emotions of despair that lingers on and on. Pain is that cause that causes me to consider. I consider my dilemma till I rediscover my purpose because my life is more than choosing the lesser of two evils. Pain is that surface. That harsh reality, that somber truth pain no matter the hurt I Still Got To Do. I can't stop now! I must move on! Huh, has that pain gone?!
(Pain) That groomed me to write this for you.

Practice Practice Practice! Till the person you dream of becomes the person you are.

I Am Alive

Day 22

There lies a moment when you just make your mind up to do something different because you need something greater out of yourself. You are tired of the same ol' same ol'. You are tired of just surviving. Something somewhere has struck a serious nerve and now you are fearfully, respectfully awake. You now vision a divine life of purpose. You now see your passion to live, love and prosper. Now you can appreciate what life is truly. Your definition of self, becomes worth.

Practice Practice Practice! Till the person you dream of becomes the person you are.

Being Better

Day 23

The harsh reality of "being Better" is the heart-wrenching discovery of "I Need to Be Better". How we treat people magnifies our deepest insecurities. Please note; there's no "getting better" until we start "getting honest" within ourselves. The relationship that establishes relationships is the personal relationship of self. Until we learn to forgive, respect and love ourselves we can't truly forgive, respect or love others. Hence "I need to be better" we must······

Practice Practice Practice! Till the person you dream of becomes the person you are.

I Celebrate Life

Day 24

I have so much to learn in such little time, I'm so excited. I can't afford to stop now. I love this life, all the UPS and downs I've experienced has made me so much greater...Even those moments that I felt like "the end" has proved to be epic turning points in my life...I'm so grateful. Though it's not perfect, it is mine and for that I am rewarded... I Am Life.

Practice Practice Practice! Till the person you dream of becomes the person you are.

I Am

Day 25

I am Fortitude! - The art of navigating fearlessly when all passes have closed in around you.

I am Champion! - The art of recovery even after defeating myself.

I am Formidable! - The art of disorientating my opponents with just a prayer.

I am Force! - The art of taking Him with me everywhere I go.

I Am A Child Of God!

Practice Practice Practice! Till the person you dream of becomes the person you are.

Practice Walking

Day 26

It's the frugal small sure-footed steps that produce the wealthiest, healthiest lives of man. Those imprints of novel have traveled the greatest journeys and has experienced the miracles in victories manifesting the unknown as now known. For this reason, I often remind myself, be humble, plan your life, live your plan and always be prepared for your next great moment of greatness is just ahead.

Practice Practice Practice! Till the person you dream of becomes the person you are.

I Am Champion

Day 27

Truth is, you are a champion, and it's never about failing or losing. As a champion, it's always about getting up. The last time you got up by faith was your last attempt at greatness. Who gets up to fall or be knocked back down... No One!!! But for whatever the reason I am down it's not reason enough to stay down, I Must Rise Again!

Practice Practice Practice! Till the person you dream of becomes the person you are.

100%

Day 28

The only way to be complete is to be absolute in all your endeavors for this is operating at 100%. Now, to function at 100 percent is to acclimate yourself, body, soul and mind to the purpose of never accepting anything less than the very best you can offer. Every task is received with enthusiasm as absolute and complete is the square. There are no more excuses for your purpose is at hand.

Practice Practice Practice! Till the person you dream of becomes the person you are.

As For Me

Day 29

I have committed myself unto self-evaluation. Even through my trial of fire I shall proof myself being that there's is no excuse or reason for me not to be the very best I have to offer. I am determined to live my purpose in spite of all the obstructions and obstacles of life. I am the foundation that makes everything better regardless of the ruins of this world. I now can appreciate all is done to make me greater. I will do all to be a blessing in this life to spread the beauty of life.

Practice Practice Practice! Till the person you dream of becomes the person you are.

The Finisher

Day 30

Making your mind up to be a "finisher" will profit you far greater then attempting to be a winner. A winner is a winner as long as he's winning. It's hard for a winner to recover from defeat if he recovers at all....but a CHAMPION! The goal of a champion is to be the greatest finisher of all time. Win lose or draw the character of a champion supersedes victory even if he loses. And if or when he loses his mental strength supersedes defeat. There will be a reckoning. I'm grateful, I've matured to be a champion. I am the greatest finisher of my time in my life. My efforts are 100% leaving nothing reserved.

Practice Practice Practice! Till the person you dream of becomes the person you are.

Nothing Shall Separate Me

Day 31

I'm intuitively motivated to be the best man I can be. Nothing, I mean nothing can separate me from the love of God! Death, murder, sickness, etc. racism, hate, violence, etc. divorce, fornication, abuse, etc. Slander, backbiting, and snares will all be refused at the gate of my very existence for nothing shall separate me from the love of God!

Practice Practice Practice! Till the person you dream of becomes the person you are.

Proverbs

Practice

Practice Practice Practice!

Make the person you dream of being the person you are.

Real

To live as a man of meekness is an attribute respected by God. A man of a meek nature has an authority ordained by God. Real recognizes real... It's better to be honored by God, for this is truly to be real. But the heart of insecurity will refuse this act of valor and will lose its purpose for naught.

The Traveler In Me

From whence I hail to my final destination So Mote It Be..........The traveler in me.

Nothing is given, nothing is wasted except for the lessons forgotten. All does well to purge me for my sacred rendezvous as I am a willing candidate fit to be pruned to the greatest man within me.

So Mote It Be... The traveler in me.

Practice Love

If power be the noun then love is the verb and my sound mind is the administrator that delivers this action to my people from black to white etc. From Christianity to Islam etc. We are all worthy of the responsibility of His power concerning one another that we love one another.

Man I am

My word is my action because my action is my word...*LOVE!*
A man of his word is a man of action. One cannot exist without the other. Power, Hope Courage and Endurance am I.

My Peace comforts me as I navigate through these lawless times. As a man, I'm pulled and pushed but my word is unchanged as my action is deliberate.

Ladders Stairs and Life

Just like ascending a ladder or a flight of stairs we must use 3points of contact. So we ascend Life, Power, Love, and a Sound Mind.

Choose your battles

I've learned sometimes it's better to look wrong and let God prove my righteousness then to fight every battle and be dead right. There is a wickedness in the pride of man that craves the blood of the brethren. Why give the devourer your life for the sake of your pride. It is truly better to be shamed for a minute and live to your greatest potential than to lose it all over what is ultimately trivial to begin with.

Footnote

The true sin is not in falling, but the blasphemy is in not getting up! We are not judged for our failures, consider a toddler as he begins to walk. Nothing gives rise when he falls down except for the gestures and help to get him back on his feet but all praise is expressed with excitement for every step taken. Now vision yourself to the Creator.

Survival

The art of survival is a story that never ends for them that survive.

The last time you survived was only a new beginning to yet survive again but the righteous desire to live and enjoy a life of abundance even in times of want. The state-of-mind of the chosen supersedes that of survival being that their existence is proved by duty and purpose.

The Gamer

To be wiser than the game (life) is the objective. However, in most cases it pays to be still and watch it all play out.

"All things work to the glory..." and the honorable trust it is so. Otherwise, it would be uncivilized to them that know, trust and love Inner-Self.

Self-Liberation

No one has the liberty to infringe on my liberties nor do I possess the liberty to infringe on the liberties of others.

As a human being my attribute is not to govern my will through your life but that I negate my fears and hold my weaknesses subject to the power within me, that I respect your liberties.

Failed Leadership

If the government fears the people they govern, perhaps they should govern with integrity rather than propaganda and violence.

There will always be more citizens than the government and moreover if the government misses the opportunity to serve its citizens that government will not govern long. The citizens are the right of passage in any strong society. Propaganda and violence throughout history have always been a tale-tale sign of a failed government…and or household.

My Truth vs. Their Facts

HERE'S WHAT THEY THINK ABOUT YOU!!!
Racism in America is the obvious but hate has no boundaries.

Truth is all men were created to be equal but the fact is, here in America those words are expressed but, the ramifications of a naivety will be put to rest. All the senseless crimes our government has inflicted and committed against the minority people of America.

The propaganda that America has sold the world concerning the minorities of America. You are challenged to study even ponder these truths versus their facts.

The Sanity of It

There is a little insanity in every sane person but, there is nothing sane about insanity.

Plan Now For Your Future

Be careful of who you are... there may come a time that you can't be who you want to be because of who you were.

Appreciate

We don't fall to our glory nor do we rise to our glory.

Everything we do is for the greater glory that we be justified as love on this earth on this day for this time.

My People
My People
My People

I Am My People

I am not color blind. I see all the beautiful colors, shades and tones of my people. I love the soft white skin of my people clear through to the deepest most intense black skin of my people. I hear and forgive the ignorance of my people. The hate, anger, and rage of my people shall not destroy my people. I accept the pains of my people. The racism, bigotry, and animosity of my people shall not engulf my people. I am a resource for my people. To them that are destitute, abandoned and left without. I will go to my people and plead the request of my people to my people. And my people being rich in charity and pockets filled with grace will bless my people for we are one people being I am my people.

I Am For My People.

What a wonderful day. Today is the perfect day to serve my people and celebrate life with my people. I love my people. Whether they be Hindu, Muslim, Buddhist, Christian etc. I love my people. I reverence my people achieving the utmost respect for my people. You see, I relish in the blessings, talents, gifts, and accomplishments of my people. I stand in awe convicted by the humanity of my people. I love my people. We are one people...I am for my people.

My People's Keeper

I am the keeper of my people. I hold the interest of my people dear to my heart. I love my people. My people are black, white, short, tall, Muslims, Christians etc.

My people are human beings. My people range from educated to uneducated even miseducated for some lbvs. They are all my people. Today I declare I have no enemies. It doesn't matter how you treat me. The profound truth of the matter is how I treat my people. I love my people for we are one people...I am my people.

Understanding

Be proud in your skin not of your skin. It's the unseen that's truly judged which is light years more tangible than the obvious. But I understand how one can confuse me for being vain in my vessel...because I wear it so well.

My Black is beautiful courtesy of the man inside.
(lbvs-*Laughing but very serious*)

Cares Of Our Mother

     The concerns and affections of a caring mother are surreal though the blood of her beautiful children run lucid in the streets are so real. Why would my people not cry out? Why would my people not expect retribution, but why would my beloved America... my people are so disrespectful. So prejudice, so bigot hearted to refuse the suffering respect. Instead, my people justified the senseless murders with more senseless violence.

     My beloved America... my people how is it that the hate in this country yet cripples you in 2015. How is it that our mother is not worth her children?! How is it that her children are not worth their lives?! And how is it armed police and vigilantes are negated concerning these crimes against humanity?! Where is the courage of my people? Where is Lady Liberty in times like this? Where is Justice... please teach me, what is law? My mother of America cries and cries and in 2015 she is yet crying for the deaths of her babies of her womb, and there is no humanity in my America to comfort her.

Woe my mother of America for your children has taken up arms and pointed them at one another. Woe my mother of America for your children have turned on one another and the streets are red with the blood of your travailing and yes there is blood on the hands of your children. May God bless you my mother, grant you peace and sooth your hallowness.

My mother of America you are the true lady liberty. The original Statue of Liberty that was given to our America looks just like you. But our beloved America could not...would not grace you. As for me, I will grace you and place you where you belong. I love you. I mourn with you. I celebrate you for your cares have been my lifeline therefore, my lifeline will be for your cares.

In remembrance to the Mothers of Martyrs.

A day in the life of…

A day in the life of…

A day in the life of…

Monuments Man

Since *before* my ancestor's enslavement I've been living and fighting for my history through clear and present danger for the future of my lineage... I am the true Monuments Man.

Distractions

Distractions are not implemented to expose our weaknesses. They are a tale-tale sign of our integrity, might, and faith.

Distractions are clever institutions that manifest our purpose. So I remind myself, *"Let not your heart be troubled, don't be distracted by the distractions... Your next great moment is at hand."*

Self can't lie to me

I have lied and I will continue to lie at one time or another for one reason or another. I may lie to my girl, a friend, my boss, police, judge and maybe even my lawyer, but in all my life, the greatest gift I've learned at a young age is Bernon...never lie to me.

Grateful

I see all things at all times, it's the truth I serve. I didn't always take heed and in most cases ignored my God-given instincts but I can honestly say "I can't say I didn't know."

Abba Father, thank you for blessing me with the wisdom to trust you. Your grace is sufficient and supplies all needs. Thank you Father for now I see.

This Moment

    Today is the first day in days since I've been able to think. As I look around me. I pause... I omit anything superficial; I must remove me from my negative self else this new day of thought will belong to naught. I have to focus, for this great moment is at hand. "Humble thyself!"

    I humble myself and rely on inner-peace, integrity, a gentle spirit and divine purpose to lead me. Because this great moment is at hand. "I step!" I move forward fearlessly. So fearlessly I walk into my destiny...The power of thought for this moment has raised me to glory. The power of thought for this moment has allowed me to prepare for the next.

Within me

Yesterday I was promised a blessing...a step up, a better position, a raise, more authority and a chance to prove who I am. But today they gave it to someone else. What a demeaning let down...smh!

But GOD!!!

Thank you Abba Father for the integrity you have instilled within me. I praise you. Your wisdom allows me to see above jealousy and covetousness. I praise You for the blessing and I thank You for my divine purpose. I am grateful for the Champion you have matured within me...the same Champion that is writing this. My purpose was created by design, and my script has been approved to His glory, so I am glorified with all that is within me.

BIRTHED NEW

One of my greatest attributes that I celebrate is my maturity. Maturity has allowed me to trust Abba Father, which birth new beginnings. Because I began to conduct myself differently.

I began to walk with authority and my words began to flow with life. His power now resonates out of me. Therefore, I say, "it's an honor to glory in the Lord for all things."

I'll build my own ladder thank you

It's not about how *we* can change or transfer ignorance to light. 2pac "let's change the way *we* think, the way *we* eat, etc..." In other words, being that *we* are here let's do what *we* need to do one for another to achieve higher ground.

Just because the system *(racism in America)* is not for us doesn't mean *we* can't be for us. It's an effort on our part to raise ourselves to our highest potential. Not because they gave us a ladder but because *we* built one.

Anew

Thoughts of new beginnings inspire dreams that procreate visions. To conclude a better place in one's mind is often the remedy to start new. Oh how I long for that moment of greatness. Oh how I welcome the breeze that stimulates my innermost.

That moment when I am one with the universe. The climax just before the pen enters the pad... Cause then the makings began. Therefore, I say "Dream your dreams, live your vision, plan your work, work your plan and live Anew.

The Light of a Man

From the experience of my life, I live my presence and prepare for my future. I consider men, women, and children according to their passion, efforts and performance. I do not possess the liberty to judge color, race, creed, or religion. My soul is too precious; My love is too valuable, and I bear witness that love indeed covers a multitude of sin. As an hourglass with wings, it's an apparent thing fleeing time. So are our transgressions removed as we establish ourselves to the greater good of one- another.

Looking to the East. Yes, modern religions were an Eastern culture stolen by Western thieves. And yes I was born in the West so yes this guilt and shame adorns even me…but please appreciate we here in the West are not all privy, so the crimes of the beast do fall on the weak. So Mote It Be!!! Rather judge me on my square.

I stand 90 degrees from the feet up, I level the breast, the elevation, and the depth of my understanding owing no man nothing but to love him. For I have knocked three times three times and was escorted by the comforts of brotherly love, trust, knowledge, and the vision of who I was to be. I and I alone journey my challenges of my life yet I know from my innermost that help is only a spoken word away.

      The traveler in me persuades me to be creative in my dealings with my fellow beings being that love is the only true thing. As a man, I bow in humility though I stand as a man. The devotion of my presence solidifies my future as power, love, and a sound mind giving surely to the cares and affections of my people in earnest, hope, and mercy. I am a bearer of light.

Psalms of Bernon

Psalms of Bernon

Psalms of Bernon

Spiritual Bliss

WoW! In all my life, I never knew there was someone out there to read me new as an open book with blank pages. I am laying here thirsty... for you.

Study me well as you become one with this picture, as I reveal to you a story of my hidden scripture. Manifest above me your heart desires, place your palms on my chest baptize me within your fire. I'm as a determined foe and you, you just keep coming. Your passion collides with my passion.

Your nails are in deep, and you look straight through me as if it hurts so good, your climax means to punish me. But I'm as a determined foe, I'm not running even though you, you keep on coming. From the looks of things it's a violent scene and no I refuse to stop because it's the principle of it all... if you know what I mean. As I anticipate your next move you counter me but I counter you and still... you just keep coming. For that moment I had you; I saw your eyes roll and did feel your soul. I had at last achieved my goal but no... not you, you just keep coming.

Enough is enough I say to myself so I reach up and grab you pulling you into myself so I can say to you "What is this thing that you do?" And she replied "I'm coming for you."

You and My Days

To wake up with you and a song in my heart is a beautiful way to start a glorious day. Seven years later you are truly greater than any dream I could have ever dreamed. From the moment I first saw you, I've loved falling in love with you. You take me to places within myself, you've taught me to love, including myself. Like a castaway left to retreat into novel beginnings. I have found all things new but complete with you. I was once abandoned but because of you I was not without. Though I was broken and left as an unhidden stain, desired of no-one, feeling helpless and hopeless as an embarrassed shame but you came along and kissed away my pains. So for all that you have given me I yield my life as a gift to you every day for the rest of my days.

Lost

I've been searching to find someone who could do me exactly how you do me my whole life. I have always known that there was one special person that would complete me from my most menial detail to my life's purpose. Without you I was lost. Now that I have you it seems without effort I am accomplishing my ambitions. My standard is as high as it's ever been, and my quality of life is next to pure. I ponder you sometimes and just gaze at us and get lost.

My Mystic Beauty

Hope anticipation space or time could have never prepared me for this rhyme. Prayer, a wish and a dream would never reveal such an untelling thing, yet a greater union has never been told. I love you my mystic beauty. That mysterious gaze that you lay upon me tugs ever so deeply you see my hidden me.

You draw me out of me into your spell searching for all of me leaving nothing of me to tell. You and you alone are the air in my sails. I've journeyed to I've journeyed fro but I have never moved, and only you know that you are my dwellings forever. I've pitched tents in dense most feared wilderness and fought death on the banks of the great abyss but only you know when I closed my eyes we were yet together me at your side cause us together is the only way I could ever survive.

My mystic beauty is my life's story as I have conquered nations she wields the glory and I am satisfied in being the honor in her eyes. Truth be told my mystic beauty deserves all of me, so I'm compelled to give myself liberally to her nothing of me is denied, and this is why my mystic beauty is mine.

UH!

Uh! I just lost myself. Sitting here looking at you has taken me to days of the past. I remember I use to be so proud of me. I recollect it being the Creator, and then the Creator created me... Yep in that order because I was sure after I was manifested there could be no other.

Then I look at you. Woman, all I have ever wanted to be is right there within you. I am all the fame that I ever desired because you are still my number one fan. I am the man on the block because you hold my hand. Woman you taught me to forgive, you taught me love. You showed what power truly was...and I'm grateful. I love this feeling. I love falling in love with you...and I'm grateful... I love this feeling.

The Thought of You

You are tracking through my mind, and I love it. Your mark is on everything within me, and I can't ignore it.

Your smile is before me in all that I do. Sometimes I just close my eyes and smile... at the thought of you.

I Love You *(A simple love song)*

The nakedness of the sky reflects the glorious mood in your eyes. A moonlit night with a cool embrace of a breeze that caresses my sweat away. Now, I'm a blessed man to witness this moment; it wouldn't mean a thing if you weren't my woman. I can love you no more than I've shown you, I've given my all to you. All I know and baby its true, I love you. I can prove it no more than I've shown you, I've given my all to you.

As the new day dawns, red rays of the sun finds me submerged in sweet streams I have drawn. I've never been better I swear this to you. I desire nothing more or less than you.

 Now, I'm a blessed man to witness this moment it wouldn't mean a thing if you weren't my woman. I can love you no more than I've shown you, I've given my all to you. All I know and baby its true, I love you. I can prove it no more than I've shown you, I've given my all to you.

Satisfied Jus-Ti-Fication

I was walking down the street man, and I saw the prettiest thing my soul had ever seen. Satisfied Jus Ti Fication!

I approached and said hi! Cause I knew I was her guy, Satisfied Jus Ti Fication! I pimped away with a smile on my face being that well …….you know Satisfied Jus Ti Fication!

So I did the math taught her my grammar and she said yeah. Satisfied Jus Ti Fication! 11 years now dawg…11 long years now damn. Satisfied Jus Ti Fication!

She told me just this morning, she picked me. I was chosen to be her man. Satisfied Jus Ti Fication! All this time I thought I won, had no idea I was just a pawn. HELL NAW I AINT SATISFIED AND AINT NO DAMN JUSTIFICATION! I been hood winked, bamboozled, I got Got…. I'll tell you! That woman got me good! Lol

…and she said Satisfied Jus Ti Fication!

Yeah!

Lol I just had to remind myself when I say yeah, its means I released *(lbvs)* Yeah!

I participated in an event that I will not soon forget. Yeah! It was one time on the beach, and I was the 'you dig,' because I was on deck... You Dig! So we are at this shindig right. Women everywhere and me being me I did what I did...right! So, I'm looking around enjoying the festivities and low and behold... YEAH!

Before I could think I had already released. I had already spoken. It was already done. So I approached her; I had to know her YEAH! (Man I did it again.) I mean she was pretty and all but, she had me in awe. There was something about her beauty that was deeper than what I saw. And when I got close enough to look in her eyes...YEAH! I couldn't even lie. There was no place to hide. She knew what she was doing to me, and neither of us cared why.

I told her; I expressed precisely what she was doing to me, and she replied YEAH! And I said YEAH! And we said YEAH, Together!

OK Daddy

I remember the first time I saw her, I didn't know her name, but I still called upon her and expressed to her that she would forever be mine, and to my surprise she replied "ok Daddy".

The first time I ever took her by the hand I pulled her close to me and I painted the picture of who I hoped to be and she looked me in the eyes and told me "ok Daddy". It's just like yesterday I can still see her face. She was the most beautiful thing I had ever seen, and I knew back then that I never wanted to leave this place and she was like "ok Daddy".

The first time I felt her kiss would be the first time I would taste her lips, *the first time I would experience her grip, the first time I would fall in love with her scent, was the first time she would hear me say "I love you woman, everything I do is my purpose for you. The picture I paint is your dream come true. Your wish is my command and with these hands I will build you your privately owned custom man. Anything you desire is my quest till I deliver because you inspire me to be a giver."*

Yes I gave her the house and she gave me a home and I reminded her years later well after the children were grown, I said "Come on woman lets go back to that place" and she said "ok Daddy"

To You

Woman I love you for my life. My feelings for you are so intensely broad and unyielding.

My Thought... Vision... Dreams of being happy begin and will end with you. Without you I could survive. I would make it but, I wouldn't want to.

Without you I would be incomplete missing the greatest part of me. It's because of your efforts that I am the man I am today. God knows the fool I use to be. Before you I was truly a fool. Woman you have blessed me in spite of your pain. You covered me with grace, never considering my selfish ways and I thank you.

But I Still Care

I don't know where you missed me at... because I know I'm a catch. It's none of my business, so you don't to explain to me your reasons…I really don't care. I'm only responsible for me and my actions that I share regardless to how I feel. I care ever so much about you, and I hope that I always will, though I clearly understand you may never be my girl... but, I still care.

You see! I'm a simple man governed by simple rules. I'm a man by myself even without you I'm still that dude. The point I'm making is, you don't have to have an explanation to suffer my heart. In my life, the times we engaged one another will forever be a beautiful part. So what I'm saying is those glorious memories that you gave to me means more to me than your reasoning for leaving me. I just want you to know… But I Still Care.

Blind Presence

Woman, if I was blind I could still see your splendor. You caromed into my blind spot, but I still feel your grandeur. I once thought I lost you in my shadow, but you are cunning and wise, you were there at my side the whole time. Resilient and brilliant, I describe you as pure. Your attentions are liberating, and your love is secure.

If I lost my mind, I would still find you. The aroma of your dignity would guide me, your virtuosity would heal my decaying conscience and deliver me again to you. I know your innermost deepest fears woman…and I have matured to appreciate those exact fears woman. I once was a fool but now I'm a man but you blessed me when I was blind it was your love that promised me I will never be blind again.

If You Let Me

Don't stop me woman, trust in me. Allow me to be the man I was born to be. Here lay your head, rest your feet you're safe now. You are safe here with me. I can conclude you're hurt. A divorced woman with children I know you're torn. I can see your pain.

Giving all your love without reciprocation can drive anyone insane. I can't imagine the cost you pay to rise to your place for every occasion. The children, school, activities and church all the cooking and cleaning woman I see your worth. I'm not here to make it worse. I'm here to put in work, imagine this. Woman if you let me I would make love to you, me being a man, then a father to your children would be me making love to you.

If you let me, I would make love to you. School, activities and church we would enjoy as a family that would be me making love to you. If you let me, your storms would be bliss, I would weather them for a kiss. I will drown your battles in the confines of my love and never consider the risk. If you let me, I will make love to you, before I make love to you, after I make love to you, I would make love to you, before I make love to you, after I make love to you, I would make love to you.... If You Let Me.

I'll Tell You What

I'll tell you what, the best day of my life was the last day of my life. That moment I knew I had never seen a star shine so bright. I had to pinch myself, shake my head. I had to wipe my eyes and repeat what I said. "I have never seen a star shine so bright".

I' ll tell you what, think about the greatest lay you ever had plus a tropical waterfall and finest woman in the world telling you she been bad. Yeah! I'll tell you what, man we blasted off, as far as I could see my eyes it seems were playing games on me. I was awake, but the whole thing was like a dream to me, if you know what I mean.

I'll tell you what, I can't even forget one scene. Like that part in a movie, you rewind in your mind. It all feels so real every time I close my eyes. I'll tell you what, I never had a heaven on earth. I never drank from paradise; this was the first. I was so emotionally and mentally discombobulated she used her defibrillator, gave me open mouth and put me right back to work as if I was being over compensated. I'll tell you what, when she asked was I coming back or could we make other plans. I said, "I'll tell you what, I will do what I can, woman I'm not superhuman I'm merely a man."

We cool

You are right, you are spoiling me. I truly care for you, but I won't grieve you when you're done toying with me. I came to you in peace and when you move on I will bid you peace. I would rather you be happily in love with your soul mate than suffer you my pain. I would rather you move on than to attempt to hold you back.

I understand we are just friends, and I'm cool with that. I have too much pride to beg or to be a stalker. I've been that way my whole life. It's the blessing of starting from nothing I guess. So whatever u do... I'm cool! We cool... U cool! Lol Be Cool.

Lustful Quarrel

The mysteries of extra relationships are defined in lust, pain, and fire. Now allow this emotion, feeling and element to marinate; Understanding none of these entities define you except for the unspoken which "love" is. Because if we discipline ourselves to love through the pain, to love through the fire; the anticipated glorious bliss of our peace will surpass and overshadow all of our bad days. For it is written "love covers a multitude of sin" and that does conclude "our sin"!

If You Love Her Let Her Go

Man have mercy on that woman, she isn't ready for your drama. You claim that she means so much to you, but you refuse her to enjoy her love for you. You know that you're not ready to settle down. Why wreck what's left of her when she learns you're messing around. Have mercy on her and bless your soul. If you love her let her go.

Man where is the grace? From the one who brags that he has been graced with so much faith. How can you treat that woman that way and say "love thy neighbor." When the love that you have for her looks more like hate and anger. Now you sing to the choir, and you already know, you can lie to her still, but the truth be told. If you love her let her go.

Man you think you're winning, but you're really simple and foolish. If she truly knew what you were doing, if she ever believed that her love for you would lead to her ruin. You would be left to stew in your sewage. That woman deserves better than that, how does hurting her make you feel like a man? I'll never know but if you love her let her go!

A man is the entity in the relationship that provides the union with hope. But you prey on the weak and destroy what's broke. Riddle me this? Being that love is complete and solidifies the deed. Being that trust is secure when all is pure, as peace is the gift, as forgiveness is the cure. What is the purpose to hurt her just because you're hurting? If you love her let her go!

I Saw Your Soul (you missed me)

All I gave you was a part of me, but you thought it was all of me. You didn't think there was more to me like I'm a tramp, like I'm a hoe, like I'm a diva pls. I'm no prima donna! I'm royalty, I'm a saint I'm an heiress of the Kemet, I reign. All woman wrapped up here in me, but you, you missed me.

I saw your soul, and I was unimpressed. As pleasant as you were to look at you're such a regret. I had for a moment considered you a man but as my luck would have it. A man of the weakest sort lesser brand. Lol! But honestly I don't judge you for being you.

I discipline myself for being a fool. I made the choice to make you better though I clearly needed to get myself together. I made the choice to love you when I should've been loving me in spite of you. But I don't judge you. I saw your soul. You missed me.

Self-Preservation

You see, it's not that I don't want you. It's just that I can't do this. There can no longer be an "us" between us anymore. "No One Has The Liberty To Infringe On My Liberties." With the intense love that I have for you. This unhealthy emotion has capsulated me here should prove my disposition. But because it doesn't, I must relinquish my plight of being with you. With you there is no peace for me in watching you steal my joy. I know you've been hurt. I know you've been wronged. But why suffer me, when I mean you no harm.

If I could, I would take you by the hand and run. I would shelter you from those things that haunt you. But my love, you are destroying yourself, you are fighting yourself. No matter what safe haven I prepare for you. Your will forever be present until you learn to love yourself. Until you respect yourself. Until you fall in love with yourself you could never love, respect or fall in love with anyone else.

Broken for Peace

The isolation of broken relationships are always stomach churning. Though it's clearly understood that the break will invoke peace. For peace sakes, I must move on. For the sake of peace, I can't look back. Feelings are the distraction that drive me off course. My feelings are like a cancer that corrupts my peace. I have learned that I must extend myself above my emotions. I have convinced myself to stop taking myself so serious. I have discovered that broken relationships are worth the break for the sake of peace.

I'm Just Saying

  The simplest thing is only as simple as it is understood. Look at the mockery we have made of love, my pilgrimage should have been ended with you...Woman. I'm Just Saying.
As a nostalgic edifice, my love will summon you to discover and rediscover the intense swells of my nature. As an obelisk at its highest peak indeed it does pierce the sky, and the revelation is received. As the geyser of the earth releases its pressure so am I revealed in that moment of our pleasure.

  The surge of our efforts exudes our passions, rich in adoration, so graphic, so lasting. Through the years, we have learned the art of agreeing to disagree. We have made some bad mistakes and would have lost it all except for the love we make, all for the sake of love. As the wonder of the pyramids of enduring time, I cast my pride aside along with its guise. I too am yet being refined. Edges rubbed smooth as a soft moon lit night. And I protrude the landscape behold the skyline is high tide. With every bit of my might I will you unto me. And again you appear, a masterpiece, a spread laid bare just for me. I'm Just Saying.

Love Story

We treat the bibles love story just as we treat our day to day relationships. We drain what we want, lust, desire out of them without committing to or regarding the responsibility of investing love for love and truth for truth.

News Flash! Everything Love did, He did it with the understanding that He was going to be murdered because of it. Every act of love, deliverance, grace, mercy and life He committed was like Him signing His own death certificate. There is no love story without a determined, forgiving, patient, loving heart. The true love story is to sacrifice... Love for Love.

Who's The Dummy Now?

Men call women "dumb dumb" and no I'm not saying women don't berate men. My point is, being a man I feel obliged to engage this dialogue into my book. We as human beings are programmed to discover love but we will accept lust because none of us want or desire to be alone, and our selfish motives will not refuse to be without even if it means having multiple partners to satisfy us as a means. But my brief point is, is it a crime that at a woman "wants" to trust her husband, fiancé or boyfriend? Because she looks over 99.9% of my extracurricular activities does not mean she is a "dumb dumb". In fact her time is honestly spent calling those things that aren't as though they are.

The truth is love covers a multitude of transgressions, and she is indeed "dummying down" to establish and prove her love. Her time of hope is spent cleaning humiliation, confusion and neglect off her face as she reminds herself to walk like a queen in spite of her brokenness. Teaching herself how to make her fake brokenhearted smile look secure and natural. Her time is painful because of the shame bestowed upon her... I'm so sorry! My Love forgive me please for being the "DUMB DUMB".

A Simple Care

The harder you make it for me to love you the easier you make it for me to leave you. The easier you make it for me to love you the harder you make it for me to leave you. It's such a simple thing, so it seems, but fairytales only exist in dreams. Will there ever be a day for respect to bare the respect of another a simple care.

So be it, the pleasantries of fantasies never submerge to reality yet we toil the legality of exploiting our love for the comforts of lust. It seems relationships might be more revealing to honor one another's feelings but that we esteem ourselves above everyone else we deal what we have been dealt in our own lustful dealings.

To scrutinize with critical eyes causes us to hide behind lies and justify the very wrong which we defy though we strategize to make it right. In lieu of it all we tumble and fall to the depths of "woe me" and subtle calls as if we were lost sheep in fear of the proverbial sharp teeth. What a telling scene.

It's such a simple thing, so it seems, but fairytales only exist in dreams. Will there ever be a day for respect to bare the respect of another a simple care.

My New Heart

Suspicion, fear and doubt I replace with grace, love, and faith. I love you woman; we are closer to the mark than we have ever been. Have courage woman and be of good cheer, have no fear for I am here.

Gird yourself to be yourself remove yourself from that dark, dusty shelf. You are the glorious entity of me, the heart of the matter the true gift indeed. The blessing of man for as long as man has touched a woman, to birth a man.

Without you woman, there could be no me. Therefore, I need you indeed as the air I breathe. So smile for me please and do your thing, you're safe here with me, for I am your peace.

My Visual

Vision you and vision me, vision us absolute and complete. Look at you look at me remember this place where we first believed. That life for you meant life for me not just for a lifetime but for eternity.

Woman I can see me touching you in places you forgot existed because no-one dared to bless you there. I can see me drifting you off into your dream cosmos, and I'll be your mulatto flying carpet because I care to take you there. Muse, my life that I yield before you will adorn your perfect creation of you. I will grace you better.

You

Captivated in the thought the new horizon has brought, an experience to treasure a dialogue of pleasure. The wealth of information achieved from conversation this ain't just recreation but grown folks relations. I'm getting high off your mind I'm hypnotized by your eyes. I'm lost within the gate of your long legged stride. From the time you walk away till you come back to me it's like I can't breathe. I can't think till you return to me. Woman you're so good you do me bad when you smile. You got me laughing at myself because I'm a fiend for your style. This wonderful feeling I don't ever want to lose this sensual healing you got me in a mood. And I know that I'm tripping but I declare to discover you. Even though we just met, I will journey till I unveil you.

Indeed It's Greater

The thought of you makes me smile, thank you. My whole life has been changed due to you. I do believe again in me; I am here for something just for me. Because of you I now remember I forgot how to dream.

The subtleties of being free have escaped me in my captivity. It's hard to remember that right now. I have allowed myself to be slow danced out of myself, leaving me by myself without myself. I forgot who I was born to be, full of zeal and spry so happy to be alive. I've been romanced by someone else for something else for the purposes of someone else, never considering I have lost myself. But you, you spoke to my heart and blessed my soul. You have soothed my pains and gave me hope.

Again I believe in me because of you indeed it's greater………………………………..Thank you.

All Cause I Flicker

Bernon: *With tears in her eyes she told me she was in love with me.)* Why must you cry I asked?

Woman: Bernon, you're the best man I ever had. You're warm and caring. You are such a good provider. You hold me down emotionally, and you're the perfect balance for my nature. You're strong and wise; your soul is like a song I sing, and I love it when you do that thing

Bernon: Do that thing? Ok, Ok if I'm all these great things why do you cry?

Woman: I love that our house is a home, I feel so special when your here but I'm secure when you're gone. I bask in what you have sacrificed for us and I love it when you do that thing.

Bernon: That thing? So why are you crying again?

Woman: *[pause]* I don't feel right telling you this.

Bernon: Ok Just say it.

Women: You make me crazy, you are so amazing I lose control. You send electricity through my body. I am crying because I can't handle the life you put into me from down there. It's like she's alive and takes over... I can't control it. What do you do to me down there?

Bernon: *[in a nonchalant manner]* Oh! I flicker.

Woman: Bernon, what is it that you do to me me?

Bernon: I Flick **Her Down There...** That's the thing I do.

Woman: and she said YEAH!

My passion...always

Woman, I just wanted to say your name. Thank u for these feelings, cares and emotions I have for you. My passion at first was just to know you. But now that I love you I just want to serve you. My passion is to adore you, bless you beyond your presence.

My passion is to honor you in your absence and celebrate you always. My passion is always for you to be secure and safe. Always, the object of my affection ever pressing my handle of affection concerning you. Always, my moment of the day. Always, the intense event of my night. Always, the one I dreamed for until I could dream no more.

My passion at first was just to know you. But now that I love you I just want to serve you my passion… ALWAYS!

When I Get A Hold Of You

When I get a hold on you, you had better understand that woman, I'm not playing with you. You better understand! When I get a hold of you, it would be wise to consider...... Yes, I will bless the obvious but the goal is to breathe life into the dreamer. Bring life to the vision that you use to envision yourself being. Since it never came true you stopped dreaming but I'm here for you. Those fantasies and expectancies that use to make you proud to be who were suppose to be. When you closed your eyes and visualize of the greatest love to be created in the innocence of your wonderful mind... am I!

Before you I lay me down I place nothing, no-one above you except my Man in the clouds. When I get a hold of you I'm going to knock the dust off you. I'm going to burn and consume the ruin of their doings. I'm going to remove old wounds I'm going to take away your bad. With peace I'm going to wash your feet and set you anew. I'm going to take a word like liberty and dress you brand new. Greater is He that is within me than he that's in the world. I be the beast in these streets, but your liberty subdues this man in me. I'm in this world but not of this world...but in our world it's just you and me girl. Your liberty is the foundation that my hope rests on. The figment of your imagination is the creation that my soul rests on. When I get a hold of you, we are going to do this thing right. Woman, when I get a hold of you, I'm going to hold you for life.

If You Welcome Me

If you welcome me, I will journey you for eternity. I will accompany you exclusively. I will honor you abundantly. I will raise you to your pinnacle, and you will summit on my horizon. There is nothing more valuable than you, there is nothing more precious than you. With you I have achieved by greatest gift. In you I've discovered my wherewithal and purpose. Understand I could never go back...I can never be without you. Woman, prepare yourself for this paradise that I have labored for you. Woman your wish is my command and you are not limited to three...if you welcome me, I will bless you eternally.

Soft As A Whisper

Your love is as soft as a whisper revealing and true falling sand for two. Your love is as soft as a whisper my strength my glow mind blowing control. Your love has invoked the mystery of my soul. It has compelled my spirit to just let go. Your love has scared and marked my heart. I'm moving fast into your arms. I'm about to crash I'm falling hard. Serenity! The settle calm before the storm. KABOOM!!!!

Your love is as soft as a whisper. It summons me near in spite of my fears. Your love is as soft as a whisper. My reason to live the life that I give. Your love, it raised me, yes I rise for you. I try to be strong, but that's all I can do. Your love, it broke the glass I'm loosed at last. I'm free to but can't move my feet. I'm going down throw in the towel. (Mayday, Mayday) Tranquility! That moment you accept that resistance is futile. KABOOM!!!

Your Love is as soft as a whisper

Smile

I can't wait for that moment when we are face to face and I make you Smile... That space that time will belong to eternity. It will be our gift to the ages. What a great sacrifice we will yield for the sake of not giving up on hope and giving love one more try. For you, Woman I will conquer my insecurities and fears to see you Smile. What I'm saying is, I Will Make You Smile!

I will make you Smile without any reservations, and there is nothing on this earth that can or will detour my journey to you. Woman.... I know we are only friends but even after you fall passionately in love with me I will still be the friend responsible for your Smile... I won't let you down! Woman I will place you where you belong in my life. My world is yours, so comfort yourself in this place we have created. Be at peace for I am your piece of paradise as your Smile is my sunrise. Be complete as we have formed one soul of two. Be at ease, you are safe here with me...SMILE

I COULD KISS YOU THERE

I could kiss you there without a second thought make your dry season flood from the passion I brought. I could kiss you there right there in your stead and stare at the whites of your eyes as they roll in your head. I'll touch you one time for the rest of our lives.

One after the other, one after the other they will never subside. A new well has sprung forth from the hidden depths of pleasure, the intense spasms the sweet taste of my treasure.

I knew you were religious, but I didn't know you were a Quaker as I minister in tongue and yield praise to your nature. I will kiss you there! You will surface my meaning. I have yet to start and you're on your third beginning. As you quiver and oblige emotion so so high, you thank God for my kiss as you bliss from inside. I will kiss you there!

Thunder!

The way you moved that thing on me is like thunder. The way you send me to ecstasy is my thunder. Just you being you doing you the way you do is like thunder. And me knowing you, being here with you to receive you is my thunder. On my back in a scene you set, is like thunder. And this sacrifice I yield to you with no regret is my thunder.

The way you beacon me when you call my name is like thunder. And the way you respond to me when you react to me when we came is my thunder. I'm looking up to see you looking down at me and I can read your chi is like thunder. A job complete we're absolutely free and you fall on me is my thunder. The love that heels is the peace that gives this chance to rebuild is like thunder. Though my greatest thrill is to know you're real and just you being here is my thunder.

All I want to do is love you

Give me some relief, won't you save me this misery, all I want to do is love you. Just to see your face adds credence to my situation, all I want to do is love you. The more of more in me tells, expression reveals within myself, all I want do is love you. Oh won't you take my hand and walk with me, I know your fears don't run from me, all I want to do is love you.

Perfection is perfected if you let it be. Forgive yourself and be who you dream to be, all I want to do is love you. I know who you are because you have broken my heart. I bare the scares yet I'm safe in your arms, all I want to do is love you. If I say that I love you would you be my man. Reciprocate my love together we'd stand. We can man this world make this earth our home. Flesh of my flesh bone of my bone, Bernon, all I want do is love you... I love you too Me!

www.ingramcontent.com/pod-product-compliance
Lightning Source LLC
Chambersburg PA
CBHW060810050426
42449CB00008B/1612